Jack and Mom

by Pauline Cartwright
illustrated by Paul Könye

Harcourt
SCHOOL PUBLISHERS

Printed in the United States of America

ISBN 10: 0-15-350608-3
ISBN 13: 978-0-15-350608-6

Ordering Options
ISBN 10: 0-15-350598-2 (Grade 1 On-Level Collection)
ISBN 13: 978-0-15-350598-0 (Grade 1 On-Level Collection)
ISBN 10: 0-15-357752-5 (package of 5)
ISBN 13: 978-0-15-357752-9 (package of 5)

2 3 4 5 6 7 8 9 10   179   15 14 13 12 11 10 09 08 07

Jack and Mom go
to the pond.

Now let's find Bill.
He has a raft.

Jack and Mom get in
the raft.

Oh, no! It will not go.

Hold on to my hand,
Jack.

Hold on to my hand,
Mom.

Thank you so much, Bill!